The Boy from Ebbw Vale

by

Raymond Hicks

ISBN 978-0-9555338-1-5
First published 2009 by Raymond Hicks
Printed by Lulu.com

*This book is dedicated to Susan,
who is sadly missed by her Husband, Brother,
and Father, and by the many people whose
lives were enriched by knowing her.*

Sweet Susan

1963–2008

Where are you now, sweet Susan?
I miss you more each day.
Your gentle image haunts me;
It never goes away.

I see you in your cradle
When you were very small,
And wonder at the joy
Your presence brought to all.

And when you were young,
Tucked safely up in bed,
Excited and eagerly listening
To the stories you were read.

I see you in your garden,
Where you loved to be:
Surrounded by the flowers
That set your spirit free.

You always brought me flowers,
When you visited my abode.
It was your way of showing
How much I was adored.

Rest in peace, sweet Susan;
No pain can come your way.
My love for you is eternal;
I think of you each day.

Dad

Contents

Acknowledgements

I would like to thank several people for their contributions to the production of this book. My son-in-law, Mike Brudenell, took the original draft and carefully read and amended the text where necessary. He then expertly transformed it into a book and created the picture for the cover. Mike's cousin, Valerie Foxon had the task of typing and editing many of the poems. My sister, Pat, and my daughter, Susan, gave me useful advice and comments that were greatly appreciated.

Raymond Hicks

odyssey@rayhicks.me.uk
www.rayhicks.me.uk

Introduction

I was born in Ebbw Vale in 1925. When its Steelworks closed in 1929 there was about fifty per cent unemployment, lasting for seven years. My father and all my male relations were either steelworkers or colliers.

Growing up in such an environment had a profound effect on me: I developed a deep fear of being unemployed.

One of my earliest recollections is of attending a primary school in Ebbw Vale. It was a small, ordinary school consisting of one large room that was split into four small classrooms after Assembly each morning.

The school is memorable to me for the following two reasons:

- In my class was a pretty, fair-headed little girl who would one day become my wife, and
- Our teacher was a lovely lady who read to us daily from the poem *Hiawatha* by Henry Wadsworth Longfellow. This was the beginning of a lifelong interest in poetry, which has given me comfort and inspiration for my long and eventful life.

I was an indifferent pupil at school, and dropped out early to work in the new Steelworks. Later, I joined the Dutch Merchant Navy as a cabin boy. My experiences during WWII slowly taught me the value of a good education.

My hope is that my autobiography, *An Odyssey: from Ebbw Vale to Tyneside,* and this volume of poems might help young people pursue a rewarding career — that my own background and experiences encourage them, especially those from a deprived background. You can find free electronic copies of my books on my web site: *www.rayhicks.me.uk*

A discerning reader will quickly realise that I am not an accomplished poet. My objective in writing these verses is to bring you some of the observations and thoughts I have experienced during my life.

Some of the contents of the book may make you laugh, some may make you cry. My earnest hope is that some of the verses will be of sufficient interest to cause you to think about some of the problems people faced in the past, and those we may have to face in the future.

Raymond Hicks

odyssey@rayhicks.me.uk
www.rayhicks.me.uk

Early Days

The Boy From Ebbw Vale

1925–

Life was very uncertain
When my grandparents wed;
They had nineteen children between them,
But in a short time five were dead.

Life gradually got better
And in nineteen twenty-five,
With luck and loving attention,
I was born at home alive.

I close my eyes and see again…
The house where my life began:
It stood at the foot of a colliery tip,
In a garden untouched by man.

I see my dad and uncle coming home,
Coal dust to their bodies clings.
To bathe they use a steel bath,
With water from a mountain spring.

Two families live in the house:
Our mothers are sisters you see.
We children are all related –
Six now, but ten to be.

With no sanitation, electricity or water
And sandstone slabs on the floor,
No roads or neighbours near us:
I guess you could call us poor!

Life in the Welsh valleys was tough then,
In the steelworks and underground.
As a result of a colliery explosion
Fifty-two bodies were found.

I close my eyes and see again…
The house where I lived when five.
I went to my first school from there:
It was hard, but I managed to survive.

The house was in a terrace for miners;
It backed on to the mountainside.
My father and siblings were born there;
With them we did reside.

I close my eyes and see again…
A lorry taking us to our first home:
To a council house in Ebbw Vale,
From which my parents would never roam.

In the first year at my school
A sweet girl came into my life.
She was fair and had pigtails;
One day she would become my wife.

This infant school was tiny:
One room daily split into four.
Our teachers were all ladies,
Whom the children did adore.

Children were called children then,
Even the poor ones with no coats.
In school we were taught that "kids"
Was the name given to young goats.

Children were taught politeness:
Like giving up a seat on the bus,
Or helping people at all times –
And doing this without fuss.

Our teachers were greatly respected,
By parents and children too.
If we badly behaved in class,
To tell our parents we dare not do.

I close my eyes and now see
Myself, at nine, in a boy's school.
All romping about in the playground
Laughing and happily playing the fool.

But our parents are not laughing:
With fifty per cent on the dole
The town had mass unemployment;
Being poor they faced a tough role.

Some with no family emigrated.
Others, like two of my kin,
Joined the army to avoid the dole,
So that a new life could begin.

It was unusual to see children
Who were classified as obese;
We played outside in the fields,
Rugby or cricket, games like these.

Diphtheria, TB and rickets
Were classmates when at school.
I was at death's door for six weeks,
But made the Grim Reaper a fool.

Friends and cousins were unlucky
A lot of them died when young;
It was a common occurrence, but
Their passing never went unsung.

We played in the streets at night:
They were safe places to be.
Children were rarely molested,
But that's how it was you see.

Fathers were steelworkers or colliers;
That is, if work could be found.
But because of mass unemployment
Many on the dole were around.

At eleven some won a scholarship;
To a grammar school they would go.
Others simply wanted a steady job:
Thus contented, did not ask for more.

I close my eyes and see mother,
Who knew we were in a fix.
She was always on her sewing machine,
Making dresses to sell for two and six.

I can also see my dad,
Sober and loyal was he.
He always had time for his children;
Both parents loved us you see.

None of my relatives were privileged
To be a grammar school girl or boy.
I succeeded in winning a scholarship,
To my parents relief and joy.

My mother was extremely excited:
She was sure I would one day be
A white collared worker in a shop –
No steelworks or colliery for me!

My joy was somewhat diminished
Since French I had to learn.
Personal feelings were quite clear:
The objective, a steady wage to earn.

Since by now the war had started
I felt that what I now must do
Was to drop out of school prematurely:
To travel and serve my country too.

My parents were very disappointed
Since they'd had great hopes for me.
But I was born with ambition
And knew what I wanted to be.

I see myself now at sixteen,
Doing the job of a grown man
In the strip mills of the steelworks:
Where my real lessons of life began.

At seventeen I left Ebbw Vale
Taking my innocent self to Liverpool –
To join the Dutch Merchant Navy;
To learn of life in a worldly school.

So I finally went away from the valley,
Where unemployment lasted so long.
Regardless how long it would take me,
I was determined to succeed and get on.

Marine Colliery Explosion

1927

When you're safely home tonight
Lying in your warm bed,
Think of the things you have –
Bequeathed by those now dead.

Think of the people of Cwm
In March nineteen twenty seven,
And the tears that they shed there
When to despair they were driven.

Early on this Saint David's day
Many people awoke in fright;
There had been a big explosion
In the Marine Colliery that night.

Life in the coalfields was tough then
And coal came at a fearful cost –
As a result of the explosion
Fifty-two lives were lost.

Think of the men who worked there
In conditions you would hate,
They simply would not have believed
They laboured to make Britain great.

Young boys were not exempted:
They too had their part to play;
In working clothes and hobnailed boots
Went down the pit each day.

Think of the wives and mothers,
Waiting at the pit head in vain,
Some nursing babes and hoping
Their men would come home again.

But their hopes turned to fear and anguish
As the relentless passing of time
Revealed the extent of the carnage
And the loss of men in their prime.

Think of the heartbroken children
Who lost their dads and brothers.
They shed many tears that day,
As did friends and many others.

But what of the men and boys below,
In that dark rendition of Hell?
Those who survived were now trapped
With little hope, entombed in their cell.

The men thought of their families,
Who would now face hardship alone.
They knew they had little time left,
And died leaving loved ones to mourn.

And what of the boys trapped below?
For them no future they'd see:
Each life to end before it began –
Why, oh why, did this have to be?

The trapped miners became fewer
As their lives slowly ebbed away;
Their cries for help became weaker –
The scene still haunts many to this day.

So when you're safely home tonight
Lying with your eyes open wide,
Think of the Marine Pit explosion
And those who, for your coal, died.

Looking for Thomas

Carmel Chapel, Beaufort 1935

I don't think I was very old.
It's very hard to tell.
One day I went to chapel
And ended up in Hell.

John and Glyn were with me,
They were my best friends;
We had been very naughty
And were sent to make amends.

Clearly this evening service
Was meant for grown-ups.
It certainly was not intended
To entertain young pups!

The preacher looked ferocious.
He liked his job that's sure.
The way he looked at we three
Made us feel we were impure.

He kept talking about "Thomas"
Who appears was not there.
We had no idea who Thomas was
And, to tell the truth, we didn't care.

He went on and on for hours,
At least that's what it seemed.
It was a form of torture,
The three of us now gleaned.

With our hands clasped before us,
We prayed to God to send
Someone to go and find Thomas,
And let this sermon end.

But Thomas was elusive.
At least it seemed to us.
For after an hour we realised
He'd clearly missed the bus.

When we got out of chapel,
To each other we did say:
"Who is this chap called Thomas
The preacher was looking for, anyway?"

Even today in the valleys
It will surely come to pass:
If you chance to meet a stranger,
He'll be looking for Thomas.

Life on the Dole

1929–1936

There's fun and joy
In being a boy,
When you're fit
And four years old.

You'll romp and play
Through each day,
Without a care
In your infant world.

But where's the joy
In being a boy,
When you're
Attending school?

With less time for play,
Throughout the day
You must study Maths,
History, and English too.

When the steelworks shuts,
There's no ifs or buts:
It's closed for seven years,
With no hope of work.

Like most of your friends,
The good time ends
When your father
Signs on the dole.

In school you'll find
Boys of your kind
Have fathers
Jobless too.

We look the same
With no-one to blame.
All have worn-out
Boots and clothes.

At least with us
There is no fuss:
A determined mother
Pulls us through.

On her sewing machine
She keeps our slate clean,
Making dresses
For poor neighbours.

Sister and I, you see,
Great friends are we.
We've always played
And stuck together.

This meant more to us
Than presents and fuss;
Though life was tough
Happy memories have we.

There is no joy
In being a boy,
When your family
Lives on the dole.

House with a View

22 Garn Terrace, Waunlwyd 1938

As a boy I lived in a cottage
On the side of a mountain in Gwent.
It was part of a terrace for miners.
There many happy hours were spent.

My joy was to sit on the doorstep,
And look across the valley to stare
At the panoramic scene below me:
None better could be found anywhere.

As part of the Ebbw Vale steelworks,
The biggest in Europe in thirty-nine,
Our house was near the heavy end,
Where molten metal was sent to refine.

From my ideal seat on our doorstep,
I could see the sparks and flame
As the Bessemer converters blew and
The pollution that from them came.

The loco pushing bogies of ingots
Emerged from the Bessemer mill;
The ingot moulds standing like soldiers,
And sparks flying to give me a thrill.

The loco from the blast furnaces
Pushing two rail mounted ladles of slag:
To be tipped opposite my first home
Were still molten, flowed with no drag.

On the other side of the valley,
Less than a mile as a crow flies,
I could see two white washed terraces
Where the main street of Victoria lies.

Prominent in this industrial panorama
Were four massive cooling towers
Continuously belching white clouds,
Each day for twenty-four hours.

To me it was a vision of wonder,
Surrounded by scenes that brought joy.
In my mind I can still see them
As they were, when I was a young boy.

The Silent Valley

1933–1973

I close my eyes and see again
The house were I once abode.
It had a back garden gate,
Opening to a mountain road.

The road was an old cart track
Made in an age long gone;
It girdled our local mountain
And seemed to go on and on.

If you left the track and climbed
To the mountain top, you'd find
To your surprise, a secret valley
Which the world had left behind.

The Welsh call it Cwm Rhydech:
The Silent Valley to you and me.
It was a piece of heaven
For people in nineteen thirty-three.

With industrial dereliction
And unemployment all around,
It was to this place I would go
To ponder the wonders I found.

On the rocks above the valley
I would often lie to hear
The singing of the skylarks,
Who overhead seemed so near.

It was from these rocks I practised
Signalling when I was a Scout:
To my friends down in the valley –
We were forbidden to shout!

Many times in my young days
I camped in the fields below.
It was very quiet and scary,
But our fear we dared not show.

In the valley there was a farm
Owned by a man named Jones.
His house was said to be haunted.
We called him Jones the Bones.

A spring on the mountainside
Was the source of a clear stream.
In the summer we built a dam
And played there, as if in a dream.

As the stream flowed down the valley
Trees appeared on its steep flanks;
These became much more abundant,
Until a wood covered its banks.

These woods gave us adventure:
Exploring and climbing trees;
Looking for birds' nests and rabbits
And other wild creatures like these.

But all good things come to an end,
At home I could no longer remain.
It was to be about forty years
Before I saw the Silent Valley again.

The vision I kept in my head
Was that I had seen as a boy.
I foolishly came to expect
A scene that would bring me joy.

What I now saw was not Heaven –
The sight on which my eyes fell
Was a huge pyramid of furnace slag
Filling the valley: a scene from hell.

When I was a boy in Ebbw Vale
Unemployment was always around,
But the building of a new steelworks
Ensured prosperity was again found.

When this steelworks finally closed,
The town once again nearly died.
When I saw the unsightly slag tips,
I just broke down and cried.

But the people of the Ebbw valley
Have always been known to be
Strong and unconquerable fighters;
And this again you will see.

Uncle Ron

Collier in Marine Colliery

One day when I awoke
To my surprise I found
A strange man in my bed,
Sleeping safe and sound.

I rushed downstairs to mother
(My distress by now had gone)
She said as she kissed me
"Don't fret, it's Uncle Ron."

Uncle Ron was a terror,
Of that there was no doubt.
He came to live with us,
To show what life was about.

He thought that in school
I was bullied, and for this
He tried to teach me boxing:
An art I must not miss.

So for my birthday I was given
Gloves for lessons to begin.
But as I was nine and he nineteen –
I could not hope to win.

To make the contest even,
He always knelt for me.
But his arms were far too long:
I could not hit him, you see.

Now Mother donned the gloves,
Wanting to have a round.
I hit her squarely on the chin
And knocked her to the ground!

This signalled the end of boxing;
With an ominous loud report
She ordered us both to find
A far less dangerous sport.

He also toughened me up
In a very unusual way:
As I reclined on the table
He pummelled me where I lay.

This had the desired effect:
My face turned a brilliant red.
The effect on Mother was frightening –
Steam seemed to come from her head.

"Look out, don't mess about,"
My Mother furiously said,
"If you keep doing that to him
His brains will burst from his head."

Many things now forgotten
Occurred during Uncle's stay.
But the one I remember best
Happened on Christmas Day…

We had some Christmas puddings
Which Mam had beautifully made
And put in some china basins –
In a cool, dark place they stayed.

Mam opened the first pudding
On that fateful festive day,
And found to her amazement
Half was neatly sliced away!

She screamed and went ballistic;
Uncle Ron and Dad turned white.
I quickly hid myself in the toilet
And stayed there till it was night.

The other puddings were opened;
The result was just the same.
It was clear the unknown culprits
Had played a cunning game.

When Mam's anger ended
A solemn inquiry was held.
Although there was no confession
Her suspicions were not dispelled.

The crime remained a mystery
To all, up to the present day.
But I believe, indeed I'm sure,
Ron knew more than he would say.

Uncle Ron was a coal miner
Like his father, and brothers too.
He joined the army to escape,
There being little else to do.

Later, when I thought of him,
I realized what he had done:
He had shown me the way to survive,
And how to look after Number One.

Tosca

Grammar School 1939

I must have been about thirteen,
That's as near as I can tell –
With a hundred or so school friends,
I was cruelly sent to hell.

Our headmaster, may he rest in peace,
Decided we were sufficiently mature
To listen to some gramophone records
Specially chosen to make us pure.

Being Welsh and fond of singing
This special rendition was to be
Verdi's celebrated opera *Tosca:*
This portion of culture to be given free.

We all sat in the assembly hall
When we were given the news that day.
I whispered to Glyn beside me,
"Who is this Tosca anyway?"

He said it was an Italian café,
Located in the valley next to us.
I somehow felt this was not so,
And prayed for the maestro to miss his bus.

Mr Brewer was to be our tormentor:
A respected and well-known radio ham.
He approached his gramophone with gusto;
His ferocity filled us with alarm.

Never in the history of classical music,
Not even since civilisation began,
Has so much pain been inflicted
On so many children by one man.

In our seats we shuffled and fidgeted.
The culture lasted two hours or more.
We silently lifted our hands and prayed,
"Please, God, show Mr Brewer the door!"

When the agony finally ended
Most children were too stiff to move.
Some banged their heads in desperation
To get their brains back in the groove.

For me the result was catastrophic:
It was years before I again tried,
To see and listen to an opera.
When I did, I could have cried.

Charlie Choppers

Have you ever been to South Wales?
If you have then you will know
That among the population there
The number of Joneses forever grows.

It's fair to estimate their number
As fifty per cent or more.
And, to prevent endless confusion,
They have nicknames by the score.

For example: the baker is Jones the Bread
And the undertaker, Jones the Bones.
But my favourite, without doubt,
Was given to Charles Llewellyn Jones.

We affectionately called him Charlie Choppers;
He was the only dentist we had.
But, certainly, not the most popular,
Particularly when a tooth had gone bad.

Now Charlie Choppers became famous
For his technique there is no doubt:
Regardless of the amount of pain, his
Solution was to pull the tooth out.

This was really not unusual
For in those days of strain and strife,
Science by then had not developed
The modern aids to improve life.

One day right out of the blue
Into Charlie's dental surgery tread
Dai Bread, the baker, clearly in pain
With a woollen scarf around his head.

"It's a molar, take it out," he cried
"Before I go out of my mind."
Charlie, with his knee on Dai's chest,
Reacted at once to be kind.

Believe it or not, but it's true,
Charlie had dropped a brick:
In his haste he extracted the wrong tooth.
To redeem himself he was quick…

To calm Dai Bread he offered
To pull out the right molar free.
This had serious national reactions,
He'd established a tradition you see.

The idea was taken up by Morrison's
As any true Welshman will agree:
If you buy a special selected item,
A second one you will get free!

If you ever go down to South Wales,
Be sure to go and reverently stand
Before a statue of Charlie Choppers,
Who's holding a tooth in each hand.

The Friends

In school, teachers believed
In Heaven they were conceived:
The inseparable Class 2 friends.

Whatever one wished to do,
The other followed too.
It was uncanny to behold.

But on a fateful day –
Why? No one at school could say –
One of the friends became ill.

Like so many at that time,
And mostly in their prime,
To diphtheria he became victim.

His parents immediately knew:
For this survivors were few,
And prepared for the end to come.

After many prayers to get well,
To the deadly disease he fell.
The young friend passed away.

The other boy knew his friend
Right to the tragic end,
Had to him always been true.

With a tear in his eye,
He looked to the sky,
And wiped it gently away.

He had known from the start
They would soon have to part.
He would never forget that day.

But deep in his mind
He knew he would find
Solace to see himself through.

With God's merciful grace
He would be prepared to face
The trials of the rest of his life.

Without divine intervention,
But with parental attention,
He grew up to be a fine man.

Now at the end of each day
In his mind he would say
To his friend, "See you again soon."

The Making of Iron and Steel

1941

On limestone, coke, and iron ore
The mighty dragon feeds,
With blasts of air and intense heat,
Enriched to meet its needs.

When the alchemy is over
And the tap hole cleared of clay,
Festooned with sparks and in haste
The liquid metal flows away.

The deslagged ladle of iron
Is carefully put to rest
In a cavernous iron mixer,
To pass a metallurgical test.

A giant Bessemer converter
Stands waiting on the ground,
With its gaping mouth wide open,
Until its liquid feed is found.

Once charged with molten iron
The converter is ready to blow.
This is done with preheated air
Through the multiple holes below.

The result is frightful and spectacular:
There's a volcanic eruption of fire
With cascading sparks and noise –
Wise workmen discretely retire.

The transformation of the iron
Results in a ladle of steel.
This is transported to a loading station,
Where teaming is done with zeal.

The ingot moulds stand erect,
Like soldiers in a row.
Then, filled with liquid steel,
To the Hot Mill they must go.

The solid ingots are now ready
To be stripped and set to go
By the gantry crane above
To a soaking pit below.

Like Shadrach, Meshach and Abednego,
They are stored in a furnace of Hell;
Until they reach 1250 Centigrade,
And taken from their white-hot cell.

The Hot Strip Mill

1941

The clanging and the banging
Of the restless slabbing mill
Signals it's now ready
To start rolling with a will.

An eight ton white-hot ingot
Is taken from the soaking pit,
And transferred by a bogie
To a short conveying unit.

The slabbing mill signals
It's waiting and ready to start.
The operators in the pulpit
Synchronise to play their part.

With thunderous manipulations
The ingot is forced to obey:
The squeezing, rolling and tilting
Which goes on night and day.

Like a massive block of butter
Being worked by a dairy maid,
The ingot becomes a 32-foot slab
To be sheared where it's laid.

With its ends neatly cropped
And, for handling, cut into a brace,
The slabs are sent to be reheated
For the further rolling they face.

The call of the mill hooter
Signals it's ready to obtain
A selected reheated slab,
For rolling to resume again.

With 150,000 horse power
The roughing mill and six stand;
Along with the hot strip conveyor,
Work with full power on hand.

Nine hundred motors are needed
To ensure the conveyor can run
At the correct speed, to carry
The strip when rolling is done.

The hot mill is half a mile long,
And the strip conveyor most of this;
To see a racing torrent of red-hot strip
Is a sight no mortal should miss.

As the steel goes through the mills
Each pass reduces its gauge.
Until the final thickness shows
It's reached the finished stage.

At twenty miles per hour
The red-hot glowing strip
Travels in speeding waves of steel,
Until a coiler ends its trip.

War Service

War Service

1942–1946

My aim, after dropping out of school,
Was to see what I could do to serve
Britain in her struggle for freedom
In a war she didn't deserve.

At this time, the newspapers reported,
There was ceaseless carnage at sea.
With little thought for the danger,
I innocently decided this was for me.

I paid my train fare to Newport.
At the shipping office I tried to join up.
The official looked with surprise at me
And said, "Sorry, lad, you're just a pup!"

I was deeply disappointed to hear this;
No doubt I looked glum and downcast.
But I soon pulled myself together,
As I'd done many times in the past.

There was no going back to school:
I'd burned my bridges you see.
So after little time for reflection,
It was clear a steelworker I'd be.

At sixteen I worked in the strip mills,
Thinking at last I was a grown man.
But this was only a boyish illusion:
It was at seventeen my real life began.

Hopefully, I went once more to Newport:
At the shipping office I tried again.
The official looked at me and said
"Too young, your journey's been in vain."

I was now more determined than ever,
And beginning to feel quite a fool.
So I gave up my job in the steelworks
And paid my own fare to Liverpool.

So I joined the Dutch Merchant Navy:
To be a cabin boy bright and green.
After two North Atlantic crossings
I doubted I'd live to eighteen.

My first trip was an adventure.
Or perhaps, I should now say,
It was a romantic misconception
Which still causes nightmares today.

This trip was a curtain raiser
To four unforgettable years at sea:
North and West Africa and France,
With more trips to New York for me.

Then three voyages to the Far East,
To India, Ceylon and Singapore,
The Hudson Bay in Northern Canada –
Who could have asked for more?

After eight ships and four years service
I found myself once more on the dole.
By now it finally became clear:
Education must now be my goal.

With no grants for merchant seamen,
I realised I must do it alone.
A correspondence course was the answer.
My lessons I could carefully clone.

My years at sea were hard going.
But on reflection I can clearly see
That the men I sailed and lived with
Helped to educate and influence me.

The Sky at Night

1942

Of all the stars in heaven
The ones I like the best
Are due to Callisto and Arcas.
To me they are twice blessed.

Callisto was a maiden nymph
Whose beauty was quite rare.
She hunted with goddess Diana
And did not have a care.

Alone one day in the forest
She was seen by the great god Jove,
Who cruelly tricked and seduced her
In a secluded, grassy cove.

Abandoned by the selfish god
She then conceived a child.
It was a boy, whom she called Arcas,
Who grew up strong and wild.

The conception angered Juno,
Jove's vindictive wife.
She planned revenge on Callisto
By ending her idyllic life.

With black malice and venom
She attacked the maiden fair,
And with her evil powers
Turned Callisto into a bear.

Arcas became a great hunter
And in the forest one day
He saw a bear, his mother,
And raised his spear to slay.

Jove was filled with compassion
And stayed the spear in flight.
Then, turning Arcas into a young bear,
Threw him and Callisto into the night.

Thus, as any sailor will tell you,
That prominent in the night sky
Great and Little Bear constellations
Can be seen with a sailor's keen eye.

In Memory of the 16 and 17 Year Old Boys of Convoys SC122, HX229A and HX229

Raymond Hicks
Cabin Boy on the Dutch Ship "Ganymedes"
March 1943

The freighters and the tankers
Rest in Bedford Bay.
All have their sailing orders
And plan to sail this day.

Fort Anne, Baron Elgin, Zaanland,
Ganymedes and *Coracero*
Set sail for dear England.
The crews all know the score.

Galley boys and coal trimmers,
Peggies, just a few.
Firemen, ABs and officers
Make up a motley crew.

Some hands come from England,
Others from far away:
Norway, Greece and Holland,
Durban and Bombay.

Muslims, Hindus and Christians,
And some with no known God;
All from allied nations,
And some you may find odd.

All tightly bound together
With only one belief:
That by helping one another
None may come to grief.

In wind and snow, they're set to go
Across the treacherous sea.
What lies below, they cannot know
The horror that's to be.

In innocence and fully dressed
They hit their bunks each night.
They dream of home and being blessed,
And then awake in fright.

The ships' alarm has sounded:
They can no longer sleep.
The young boys are confounded:
They have their rules to keep.

With sleep-starved eyes
And lips sealed tight
They scan the ominous skies
Before the perils of the night.

They cannot see the Wolf Pack,
The silhouettes are too low.
They know they cannot turn back:
There's just nowhere to go

A deafening explosion
Means a freighter has been lost.
Some men are in the ocean;
They're about to pay the cost.

Their lifebelt lights are blinking;
Their shouts are loud and clear.
We know they will be thinking:
There is no rescue near.

Five minutes they are given
Before they freeze to death.
They're on their way to Heaven
With one last worldly breath.

A thunderous ball of amber
Rises quickly in the sky.
"It's from a crippled tanker,"
We hear our shipmates cry.

There's little hope for the tanker's crew:
The sea's a roaring fire.
The price that's paid by the few
To sate man's war desire.

The carnage continues three more nights
Till air support's in range.
Aircraft with their long haul flights
Herald a welcome change.

The only things against them now
Are the hurricane winds and cold,
And treacherous seas of ice and snow.
By fewer men the tale is told.

The final cost was taken:
Twenty-two ships had been lost;
As well as many crewmen.
A shocking, dreadful cost.

It's the price that's paid for petrol,
Sugar and meat and bread,
Guns and planes and tanks and oil –
For Britain must be fed.

But the story is not ended,
For in a week or so
The ships will be directed
To cross the sea once more.

The Story of Ali Adhem

Shipmate from Tiger Bay

Ali was a seaman
Who came from Tiger Bay.
He's rather bent and slow now,
And his hair has turned quite grey.

At ninety-one his life's near done,
He could not have asked for more.
With wife long dead, it is said,
He too must settle his score.

He finds no mirth in being on earth,
He knows God's laws are plain.
He's had his fun around the world,
And will never see Bombay again.

He opens his mind to see the past,
Which comes back loud and clear.
He sees a boy of sixteen years:
Happy and bright, without fear.

He joined a ship in Cardiff docks,
What else could he have done?
He became the fireman's Peggy
On board the *Port Cadoxton.*

At eighteen he was a coal trimmer,
A hard and dangerous job it's true.
Then progressed to be a fireman,
An important part of the crew.

Before war came he was married,
To an Indian girl named Sari.
They rented a flat in Bute Town,
Their twosome soon became three.

His trips now became uncertain;
Nobody knew where he went.
Very soon he was torpedoed, and
Many crew to Heaven were sent.

In panic, with pleas made to Allah,
He finished alone in the drink.
Grabbed by his mates in a lifeboat,
He was saved before he could sink.

Seven seamen where in the lifeboat:
Four Christians, two Muslims, one Jew.
There would have been room for others
But these were the last of the crew.

Thirty and more are in Heaven.
Or maybe some are in Hell:
It's hard to say with a seaman,
And only the Lord can tell.

In battle men die in their thousands
But in a lifeboat this is not done.
No food, no drink, in rain and cold:
They just die one by one.

That is, all except Ali,
Who did not succumb like the rest.
He lived to tell his sad story:
Perhaps he was by Allah blessed.

Tiny Lights

For Bobby Clubb, friend and shipmate

With hurricane winds gone,
Calm returned to the troubled sea.
Although constantly wet and cold
More confident the crew could be.

One night, when least expected,
A terrifying explosion rent the air.
A ship had been torpedoed;
We could only stand and stare.

It was an ancient freighter,
With a general cargo of food:
Destined to feed starving Britons,
And chosen to do some good.

Forty seamen were doomed,
To close their account that night.
Engine room firemen and trimmers
Were fully aware of their plight.

Toiling below the waterline
They only had seconds to live.
With seawater rapidly rising,
Their lives they would give.

The surviving crew members
Jumped into the freezing sea.
With no time to launch a lifeboat,
Lifebelts would their only hope be.

Each lifebelt had a tiny light,
For would-be rescuers to see.
But no ship was allowed to stop,
So no rescue could there be.

Each tiny light in the dark ocean
Marked a spot for a seaman to die.
They all knew they had five minutes
To see, for the last time, the sky.

The captain, like the rest of his crew,
Desperately fought to survive.
But he knew his wife in Liverpool
Would never again see him alive.

Some of the crew prayed to Allah
And some to a Christian God above.
Others thought of the girls they'd had,
Who freely gave them their love.

The boy ratings in the water,
Whose lives the sea would take,
Thought of their mothers and sisters
And the hearts they would break.

They went to sea for adventure.
But for them no future they'd see.
Each life to end before it began –
Why, oh why, did this have to be?

The little lights became fewer
As we continued on our way.
The cries for help became weaker.
The scene haunts me to this day.

Ben and Kim

Ben and Kim were both sixteen,
Born on the same day.
Ben came from the Welsh valleys,
Kim from the slums of Bombay.

Ben was brought up a Christian,
Kim a devout Muslim.
With their different religions
Could Ben be a friend of Kim?

Ben had seen much hardship
With his father on the dole,
And his mam found it difficult to manage
To keep the family whole.

Kim was born into poverty
On the crowded streets of Bombay.
He slept each night on the pavement,
As many do still, to this day.

By fate or heavenly intervention,
Ben and Kim found one day
They had both signed on a freighter
To stay on as long as they may.

Ben was engaged as a cabin boy,
Not a very hard job to do;
And Kim was the sailors' Peggy:
A very good task for him too.

They both lived in the fo'c's'le,
With eight or more seamen.
Their first trip was to New York,
Which excited Kim and Ben.

With ferocious winds and always wet
They faced the ice and the cold.
"Don't worry boys we'll soon be there,"
They were constantly told.

As each day passed their luck held firm,
But with a thousand miles to go
There was a thunderous explosion,
And their freighter was no more.

A torpedo had struck amidships
And most of the crew were lost;
Only Kim and Ben survived,
In the sea at a fearful cost.

The ship was to load in America
Three thousand tons or more
Of food and vital war supplies,
Which Britain must now forgo.

But what of our teenage Kim and Ben,
With no hope of rescue in view?
The policy was to leave them alone:
It was too risky to stop for so few.

With no chance in the icy water
They had five minutes to live;
Clinging together for comfort,
They had no more to give.

Then on the breath that men call death
Their spirits were borne away
By the same God for Ben and Kim,
To peaceful rest far away.

I like to think their lesson,
For men of faith and none,
Will shine so strong on our last day
And all conflicts will be done.

Because, not to beat about the bush,
When it comes to the mystery of life
And when our chips are about to fall,
What cause is there for strife?

What We See

1942–1946

Looking at a newsreel
What we really see
Are images of the past,
Retrieved for you and me.

The pictures may relate
To scenes of yesterday,
Or events that happened
In places far away.

Our minds are accustomed
To information like this,
But there are some images
Whose significance we miss.

Looking at the night sky
I can see the Great Bear,
But I cannot be certain
That in fact it's really there.

If the Big Bang happened,
Then what we see at night
Depends upon its remoteness
And the finite speed of light.

To me it seems possible
That the images we see
Are of stars that existed,
But by now have ceased to be.

The time that light has taken
To reach our earthly eyes
May be more than that needed
For the star to finally die.

Inside My Mind

I don't know why it should be
But locked within my mind
Are endless lists of questions,
Whose answers I can't find.

They're there when I'm out walking
In a lonely street at night,
Or when I'm in my bathtub –
It surely can't be right!

It happens when I'm fishing,
When fish are hard to find.
It doesn't really matter,
With questions on my mind.

Or lying on a mountain,
With skylarks up above.
I'm never really lonely
With questions that I love.

In school I was taught
There's one God up above,
And of His many virtues:
The greatest one is love.

But Ali in our fo'c's'le,
Whose bunk was next to mine,
Had a different conception
About the word "divine."

Another view was held
By my friends in fair Japan,
And also by those in India
Where my serious doubts began.

For me it posed the question:
Can they all be right?
I can't give a sure answer,
But conceivably they might.

My mother's views were simple:
That in our mortal span
We should leave this world a better one
Than when our lives began.

Words of Warning

The Creator of all Life,
God to you and me,
Decided that earthly strife
No longer can there be.

So He conceived a plan
To end this sad affair:
He chose from every clan
A human His views to share.

The wisest of the leaders
Of each sovereign state,
Philosophers and teachers
From now or earlier date.

He also chose believers
From every known religion;
Imams, Rabbis and Priests –
Their variants were legion.

God then held a convention
Of all those mentioned above,
And to every man and nation
Said to them with love:

"About two million years ago,
Or perhaps a little less,
I put on earth to forego
An upright man to bless.

"I gave him a brain to use
To solve the problems he met.
This he was not to abuse
And give me cause to regret.

"I created for him the Earth
To satisfy all his needs,
With seas full of fish to eat
And plants with abundant seeds.

"Beneath the ground I provided
The minerals to keep him warm,
And those to be fashioned into tools
To keep him safe from harm.

"I gave him birds and animals
So he would never be forlorn;
They were to be his brothers.
He had no reason to feel alone.

"All was going well until
He learned to read and write:
Not many people on earth still,
But they had learned to fight.

"I do not quite know why:
Perhaps I must have blinked,
Or my mind was on the sky
Where new stars I made winked.

"But this I can tell you,
Believe me I never lie
Of this you can be sure:
All men will one day die.

"They may die as a race,
Or just die one by one.
All will go to the same place,
When life on earth is done.

"Let me be frank and honest –
In the great mystery of life
When you're near your final rest:
There is no place for strife.

"Conflict in religious views
Can only bring more hate.
So reject conflicting reviews,
Let peace be man's fate.

"Forget the laws of nature then,
Of physics, maths and time.
Create your personal Eden
In the regions of your mind,

"Some may be in doubtful bliss
And wonder if this is true.
My final observation is…
It all depends on you.

"The day will surely come
When life on earth will end:
By destruction caused by some,
Pursuing their selfish ends."

Life on Earth

I find it thought provoking,
And maybe you do too,
But it is generally accepted
And the natural thing to do.

Of all the living creatures
The greatest by far is man,
And this has been the case
Since human life began.

Now I have great difficulty
In accepting this intact:
There seem to be anomalies;
Some assumptions are not fact.

Take man's basic senses
And compare where you can:
For each one you consider
There's an animal in the van.

For sight it is admitted
That an eagle can easily see
Further and much clearer
Than either you or me.

Many creatures in a forest
Can hear much better than man –
So ask yourself this question
And answer if you can.

Did God make man in his image?
It seems an odd thing to do.
Or did man, because of conceit,
Imagine God to be like man too?

There is one special sphere
Where man is supreme for sure:
That's his destructive nature,
A fault impossible to cure.

One thing at least is certain:
It's that the day will surely come
When life on earth will end,
By the ruin caused by some.

Education

Education

“There is no fun in being twenty-one,
If you’re out of work on the dole,”
My mothers’ words came back to me;
I must now find a new role.

The Resettlement Board advised me:
To succeed in life, although I’m late,
I must study at home by correspondence
For a University of London Certificate.

The Employment Officer was helpful –
It appeared I had reason to rejoice:
It was either a job with the fishing fleet,
Or be a builders’ labourer by choice.

To study at home was important,
So a builders’ labourer I chose to be.
Thus I began a correspondence course,
Which lasted over a year for me.

I started work on a building site,
A pick and shovel were my tools.
My job was digging ditches,
With labourers who were no fools.

After some time I was lucky:
With the help of a great friend
I got a job as a trainee civil engineer,
So my labouring came to an end.

The job was on an opencast coal site
On top of a mountain in South Wales.
There I learned a lot about geology,
From the fossils I found in the shales.

I was taught to do site surveying
And learned a great deal of maths.
I mastered all this quickly,
Clearly I was on the right paths.

McAlpine my employer was helpful,
They sponsored me one day a week
To attend classes at a Technical College
For engineering knowledge to seek.

I studied for a National Certificate,
For this I worked hard to secure.
I also continued my home studies,
To matriculate I had to be sure.

Since I was doing well at the College
My lecturer one day said to me
I should try for a University scholarship
So, if successful, I would get a degree.

By now I had a sweetheart,
Who agreed I should study yet more;
She was sure I had the ability in me
To reach a higher academic score.

Her faith in me was rewarded
For in the summer of forty-eight
I won the University scholarship –
To get married we would have to wait.

With a University place secure
I had to decide where I would go.
The obvious choice was Cardiff;
To alternative venues I said "No."

Nine long hard years were needed
To study and reach my goal.
With good academic qualifications,
I had no further fear of the dole.

The Vision

It may sound unbelievable
But I assure you it is true:
I really live in two worlds –
I'm sure you do too.

As well as the material world,
I've locked within my mind
A wonderful world created
Of a very personal kind.

I demonstrate this each night
When I'm snugly in my bed.
As I relax and close my eyes
These thoughts enter my head.

I leave my body and settle
My mind on a photon of light.
Immediately I leave the earth
And traverse celestial night.

Time to me has no meaning;
I have no material weight.
You see I'm only a thought –
The feeling is simply great.

I pass many stars and comets
Until I come to my goal –
I finally see my objective:
It's the centre of a black hole.

I'm not at all worried about
Singularities and infinity;
Since I'm now only a thought,
I've no need of help or pity.

I emerge from the black hole
To a blazing vista of light;
All space has an ethereal glow.
I sense no need for fright.

A big crowd of people I see
Throughout a heavenly space.
It's clear they're from history,
Representing every known race.

Some are famous scientists
Galileo, Leibniz and Newton.
Others great philosophers like
Plato, Socrates and Bergson.

At a prominent spot on a dais
Where it is easy to be seen,
Is a large table with chairs –
I have counted seventeen.

At the head of the table is
A magnificent empty throne;
"There's to be a big meeting,"
People murmur in a low tone.

At last a regal procession
Comes slowly into life;
The members are very friendly,
They give no sign of strife.

It is slowly led by Abraham
With his illustrious kin;
Then Moses, Mohammed and
Jesus – brothers under the skin.

Then comes Confucius
And people from other races:
Celts, Japanese and Indians –
They have distinctive faces.

Now Abou Ben Odhem arrives.
He sits on the golden throne.
On earth he did not know God;
It seemed he loved man alone.

Abu Ben Adhem was chosen
To receive the heavenly call;
God had singled him out to be
Important to Him above all.

The Cabinet was brought to order
To consider one problem, no more:
It was that the earth was in danger
Of war, caused by man as before.

The subject had been debated
By the Cabinet in the past,
But now it was clearly obvious:
This chance would be the last.

The world is far more dangerous
Than it was when I was a boy:
With weapons of mass destruction
And atom bombs they could employ.

With supersonic war planes,
Intercontinental rockets too,
Some with nuclear war heads
Our annihilation they could do.

The Cabinet jointly concluded
That carnage there must not be.
But they faced an obvious fact:
To enforce it, they could not agree.

The United Nations were asked
To step in and jointly act.
But from past experience knew
They could do very little in fact.

In desperation the Cabinet
Threw up their hands in prayer,
Asking God to intervene for them
But to do this He did not care.

It was now perfectly clear
For there to be peace on earth,
All the nations of the world
Must pursue it for all its worth.

So forget your national pride
And your selfish interests too:
For the sake of your children,
And their children, it's all up to you.

The Golden Key

There is a golden key;
It opens any door.
For you it comes free –
No need to ask for more.

The key is your own will,
Which can be used to place
Ideas in your mind, to fulfil
Ambition's marathon race.

Do not be down hearted,
If you are old and grey –
The magic can be managed
To get you on your way:

On the road to succeed
In the challenge of life;
No need to intercede
By conflict or by strife.

Do not be discouraged
If you feel you are too poor;
Remember the deprived aged
Who opened the closed door.

Lincoln and many more
Were born to poverty too;
Self educated they opened the door
And showed the way to you.

They opened the door to fame,
And sometimes riches too.
Not interested in blame,
They started just like you.

Do not count your wealth
By the money you have got;
But value your good health:
This is always worth a lot.

Also, while you're at it:
Include your good friends too.
Because they clearly merit
A great value given by you.

Do not be over obsessed
By material things alone;
Remember you are blessed
And have no cause to moan.

The status of your birth,
And the colour of your skin
Do not affect your worth,
Or thoughts you have within.

Not the riches that you have
Nor the silver spoon you own;
Your future they may save,
But not give you a crown.

To open up your doors,
The golden key is this:
Education found on two floors –
These you must not miss.

The first teaches you about life;
The second about a rewarding career.
These can be had with honest strife,
With them there is nothing to fear.

Learn about life and your prospects
From parents and others you meet;
Be sure you study the right subjects
To be certain poverty you defeat.

Think

When you're safely home at night,
Perhaps lying in your bed,
Think of all the things you have,
Bequeathed by those now dead.

Top of your list are sure to be
The gifts of freedom and life;
Both of which were costly,
And only achieved through strife.

Think of your parents and others,
And their antecedents too.
I know this goes back a long way
But they all gave something to you.

The adults and children who worked
In conditions you would hate;
Surely would not have known
They laboured to make Britain great.

Think of the old ones around you:
Some will have served in the war
With comrades who stood with them,
Who gambled and lost in the draw.

Some will be over eighty
With little more time left to live,
So when you see them disabled
Think of what you could give.

Think of the many people
Who've helped you on your way,
And those you worked and lived with
Who advised you day by day.

Think of your teachers at school
Who taught you from books they read:
To educate and prepare you
For the trials of life ahead.

But most of all through your life
Remember this little known fact:
Not all the things you are told are true,
So think carefully before you act.

Of all gifts given to man
One of the finest it's true
Is that of using your own mind
To let sense and wisdom accrue.

Don't worry about your beginnings,
Your future belongs only to you.
Work hard on your dreams and ambitions:
And remember, it's all up to you.

Advice on Choosing a Career

The Boy (or Girl)

What can I do when I grow up?
This is a great decision for sure!
It must be rewarding, steady and safe,
But what job will these secure?

Some aspire to being a doctor:
A noble profession it's true.
Others would a surgeon be,
For which respect is also due.

Personally, I cannot bear the sight
Of seeing people in pain.
Although I fully realise
They restore good health again.

There is the study of commerce,
Which covers so many fields:
Banking, accountancy, and trading –
With their lucrative monetary yields.

But for me they somehow lack
The challenge that I now seek;
I'm looking for something that
Will satisfy my creative streak.

The Old Man

Perhaps I can help this boy (or girl)
Since I've travelled the career road.
I'm now over eighty you see
And have much experience stored.

When war service ended in forty-five,
I started on a great adventure
As a civil engineer with McAlpine,
To a rewarding and exciting future.

By getting academic qualifications
My civil engineering career began:
A nuclear power station for Scotland,
An earthquake proof one for Japan.

Then interesting work in industries
Such as steel, building and coal:
With visits to many sites overseas,
Before I reached my final goal.

As MD of a company on Tyneside
I could now genuinely claim,
That my choosing civil engineering
Was an exciting and rewarding aim.

Now the trick of success is to know
What your profession is to be;
There's no point in years of study
If you get an irrelevant degree.

Regions of the Mind

Do not be downhearted
If you fail to find
The things you dream and pine for
Are constantly denied.

Kipling, Gray and Goethe
Knew the road quite well,
From barrack-room and graveyard
And Faust's long road to Hell.

Beyond the realm of reason,
In a region of your mind,
Resides the road to wisdom
Which some folk cannot find.

It cannot be detected
By sight or sound alone
It lies in isolation
When you are safe at home.

Or lying on a mountain,
With skylarks up above,
And thinking of a problem
You cannot solve by love.

Or casting in a river,
With nothing on your mind,
Except the need to ponder
Which fly the fish will find.

So do not be contented
With material things alone.
There is a world to conquer
Which nature cannot clone.

Forget the laws of nature,
Of physics, maths and time.
Create your personal Eden
In the regions of your mind.

Male Voice Choir

1948

When your toil is over
And the skylark's on the wing,
Lift your heart to heaven,
Loosen your belt and sing!

Sing of the Hebrew slaves,
Returning home from Babylon:
Of their hopes and longings
As they sang and journeyed on.

Sing of joy for Tannhäuser,
When again his friends he meets,
After his long penitent pilgrimage
And once more his home he greets.

Sing of the long ago martyrs
Who in the arena once fought.
They only gained their freedom
With a life cruelly bought.

Sing of Astrid the Abbess
Beseeching at praying time;
Alone in her chamber at night,
In the convent in Drontheim.

Sing of the Jolly Roger,
Going off to sea for fun;
Then chasing the Spaniards
When the Jolly Roger's hung.

Sing when you're in your bath
After a long days work is done,
Or when you're in the shower –
You'll find this is great fun.

But don't sing on the bus,
You'll regret it if you do:
The passengers will turn round
And look with sympathy at you!

The important thing to remember,
It's simple you will agree:
That by constantly singing
Much happier your life will be.

The Match

In Memory of Peter Clubb

I remember the day quite well:
A Saturday just after the war.
Ponty was playing Ebbw Vale;
Supporters came from afar.

The weather had been dreadful;
For this we had no care –
The only thing we thought about
Was, will those Johnnies be there?

There had always been a feud
Between these two sides, they say.
Nothing really vicious mind
Except, perhaps, on Saturday.

No one knew how it started,
Or what it was all about;
But it always resurfaced
At the annual rugby bout.

The teams came onto the pitch,
Each from a different gate;
They dare not come together,
The danger was too great.

Steam came from their bodies
Before they started to play;
They were clearly well worked up,
We would never forget this day.

As they lined up in the middle
The ref, who didn't want to die,
Retreated to the sidelines for safety.
The ball was kicked into the sky.

The Ponty fullback was fearless:
While he bravely stood his ground
Fifteen charging men engulfed him –
He disappeared without a sound.

When the attacking players parted
And the pitch was cleared of steam,
They were all covered in thick mud
And the fullback was nowhere seen!

He'd been overcome by the pressure
And was pushed into the ground;
His imprint was distinctive and
He took some time to come around.

His injuries were not serious:
Just bruises and blood it drew.
He did however lose some teeth,
But in minutes was as good as new.

The game continued for ten minutes or so,
With no injuries serious enough to mention,
Although Dai Boot had a cut on his head
And the Ponty scrum half concussion.

The crowd were clearly enjoying the game:
They kept jumping up on their feet.
Spectators from both sides were mixed
But with them, no aggression you'd meet.

The players were also enjoying the game,
You could clearly see this was true:
There had been little fighting on the field –
Just a few punches, and a kick or two.

Then a slight mishap on the ground
Resulted in an undisciplined scrum.
One man had a piece of his ear bit off,
And two others were bit on the bum.

None of this was important,
But suddenly there was a shock to all.
It could now be seen that the players
Were carrying on with no ball.

"Forget the ball, carry on with the game,"
The spectators repeatedly shouted aloud.
The players knew what had happened
And played on to satisfy the crowd.

With a new ball, they all changed ends
This was considered to be just fine.
It was a great help to the home side,
Since the bar was behind the Ponty line.

Both teams played like demons
For their pride, as you can see.
They were so covered with mud
That everyone could an opponent be.

It was clear the game was nearly over
By the way the crowd began to sing:
Bread of Heaven and *Cwm Rhondda*,
And ended with *God Save the King*.

The final whistle now sounded;
It gave real trouble to them and all.
It was caused by a disputed goal –
Which side of the post did it fall?

With Ponty 22 and Ebbw Vale 21
It was vital all should agree:
That the ball had dropped inside
To give the home side victory.

In the dressing room sharing a bath
The two teams diligently tried,
To settle the dispute with logic
But clearly they could not decide.

Before the end of the day
Four ambulances visited the ground.
The injured were taken away
With signs of disagreement around.

Now if in the future you find
You go to Ebbw Vale for a drive,
Don't raise the topic of the match
If you want to leave Ebbw alive!

Industry

Industry

Now I had to start a career.
It was not hard to choose:
I decided on Nuclear Power,
With this I could not lose.

Our Atomic Energy Company,
Was established in Erith, Kent.
A design for a nuclear station,
To a Scottish client was sent.

The basic design was accepted,
There was still a lot to be done:
Design details and stress analysis –
It was demanding, but great fun.

We then won a second order:
A nuclear power station for Japan.
This was to be earthquake proof;
On this design work began.

Since I was considered an expert,
On stress concentrations in plates
It was clear I would be travelling
To Japan on many future dates.

I made good friends in Japan,
Whom I regularly went to meet
To study earthquake regulations:
There were many problems to beat.

After five years I became restless:
To me trouble seemed imminent.
We were running out of orders
And I could be made redundant.

I looked around for a new job,
And after some research found
A position with Head-Wrightson
On their Teesside home ground.

My interest was mainly steelworks,
Which was very near my heart.
All this was very interesting,
But after two years had to part.

We loved the North-East of England,
Particularly the Moors and sea.
But we knew we must be practical:
It was down South we had to be.

I became Group Technical director,
With subsidiaries amounting to ten;
The Group was Winget Gloucester,
My job meant visiting them often.

As I had dual responsibilities
In Gloucester and also in Kent,
After two years of commuting
To Rochester we finally went.

Our company was now in crisis:
We were taken over it seems
By Babcock International –
This may be the end of my dreams.

After a short time for assessment
Babcock decided to transfer me
To Huwood, a Tyneside company:
The Managing Director I was to be.

The company was famous in mining:
Underground equipment their trade.
Its main customer was the Coal Board.
At last my objective had been made.

With a workforce near two thousand
Its equipment was globally found.
I travelled to many countries
Where coal was found underground.

I got on well with the Geordies:
We had a lot in common you see…
I was born and bred in the Valleys,
Coal mining was well known to me.

Marjorie's health became a worry.
So I took retirement at sixty-two.
She died too soon in her sixties.
I now needed something to do.

Retirement

With Marjorie gently put to rest
And my children living away,
I finally found myself alone
In an empty house to stay.

But with my imagination
I always feel she's at my side.
My children visit me regularly
And good friends near abide.

Although I think about her
I've very rarely grieved,
But thankful for the years
Happily together we received.

Looking back over many years
It's very clear now to see
That all my live I've been lucky
By the way she supported me.

I've had fifteen years of fishing,
Painting and other interests too;
With many friends around me
I'm never short of things to do.

I've travelled the world over:
Bombay, USA and Port Said.
But after thirty years on Tyneside,
I'll stay here until I'm dead.

But my heart has always been
In the valley where I was born:
With memories of happy days
And the joyful times now gone.

In the Memories of my Mind

1930–1991

I see a little girl
Walking lazily to school.
She's fair and very pretty,
Her hair a golden pool.

Her hair is now much longer
And a pigtail I can see.
We're in school for Christmas
And at a party she picks me.

Now I wear long trousers,
I'm growing up quite fast.
We are mutually attracted
And it's clear it will last.

Dark clouds fill the horizon
And I feel that I'm in hell;
Will this war go on forever?
Not one of us can tell.

By know I'm twenty-one
And held to be a man.
I see that little girl again,
As she was when it all began.

Our attraction is still there,
Stronger now than ever.
I must go away to study
But her loyalty lasts forever.

For four long years apart
She waited, as she said.
I see her clearly now
On the day we finally wed.

Through forty happy years
We lived our lives together.
For our two lovely children
She was the perfect mother.

Her life was rendered hard
By perpetual poor health
But by her shining presence
She gave us all great strength.

She died much too early for us,
As colour fades from the trees,
Leaving us alone and sad –
But for her it meant release.

But in the memories of my mind
She's always at my side:
There at dawn and then at dusk…
For me she's never died.

Keeping Fit

2008

I don't know were I'm going,
And don't know where I've been.
Nor do I know what day it is
Or remember whom I've seen.

I cannot find my glasses:
I've put them down, I suppose.
My sister takes one look and says,
"They're hanging on your nose!"

I never know which day it is
(I've stopped the Times, you see).
Appointments are inscribed with care
In my diary… but where can it be?

Every day I take my tablets,
That is, if I don't forget.
It's a comprehensive cocktail
And they form a colourful set.

They combat my blood pressure,
Protect my failing bones,
Help my indigestion and give my
Muscles supple tones.

In spite of all these problems
I assure you I'm quite fit:
Today I'm going walking…
But not till I've kipped a bit.

No matter what I say or do
I don't want you to think
That I am getting senile,
When I'm really in the pink.

There's every reason to believe,
If I'm careful and turn up the heat,
I'll be around for quite a while
And outlive Coronation Street.

Eternity

Beyond the outmost planets
In space unknown to man,
Is a place of mythical magic
Conceived when time began.

It cannot be seen or reached
By any known earthly means,
And is specially reserved
For our thoughts and dreams.

When our time on earth is over
And we get a well-earned rest,
We leave our material bodies
For this place forever blessed.

Time there has no meaning,
Nor does colour creed or race.
There is no pain or suffering.
Of hate, there is no trace.

Our earthly time is finite,
And sometimes hard to bear,
But each life will end one day
Then "ETERNITY" with no care.